MASTERING

YOUR

MONEY

A Comprehensive Guide to Financial Success

RENU EKKA

Mastering Your Money

Table of Contents

Introduction:

Mastering Your Money

Welcome to "Mastering Your Money" – a comprehensive guide designed to empower you on your journey to financial mastery. In the pages that follow, you will discover practical tips, insightful lessons, and real-world examples that demystify the intricacies of personal finance.

The Need for Financial Mastery

In a world where financial landscapes are ever-changing, mastering your money is not just a luxury; it's a necessity. Whether you're starting your financial journey or seeking to enhance your existing financial knowledge, this book is your roadmap to understanding, managing, and ultimately thriving in the realm of personal finance.

Unlocking Financial Potential

"Mastering Your Money" goes beyond traditional financial advice. It delves into the nuances of budgeting, investing, debt management, and more. Each chapter is crafted to provide you with actionable insights that you can apply to your unique financial situation, helping you unlock your financial potential.

Practical Lessons and Real-World Examples

The power of this guide lies in its practicality. It doesn't just provide abstract theories; it offers tangible lessons and real-world examples that illustrate the application of financial principles. From setting and achieving financial goals to navigating the complexities of taxes and investments, you'll find practical guidance for every aspect of your financial life.

Your Personal Financial Journey

Recognizing that personal finance is indeed personal, "Mastering Your Money" empowers you to tailor financial strategies to fit your goals and circumstances. Whether you're looking to build an emergency fund, invest for the future, or navigate the intricacies of credit, this book provides the tools you need to craft a plan that aligns with your aspirations.

A Comprehensive Guide

This guide is not just about managing money; it's about mastering it. Each chapter builds on the previous, creating a comprehensive framework that guides you from foundational financial principles to advanced strategies. By the end, you'll possess the knowledge and skills needed to navigate the complexities of personal finance with confidence.

Your Financial Future Starts Here

Embark on this journey with an open mind and a commitment to your financial well-being. "Mastering Your Money" is more than a book; it's your companion on the path to financial mastery. As you turn the pages, envision the financial future you desire and know that every principle you grasp brings you one step closer to that reality.

Here's to your journey of mastering your money – a journey towards financial empowerment, security, and the freedom to design a life aligned with your dreams. Let's dive in!

Mastering Your Money

Chapter 1:

Foundations of Financial Wellness

Lesson: Understanding the Basics

Welcome to the foundational chapter of "Mastering Your Money," where we'll embark on a journey to understand the fundamental concepts that underpin financial success. By mastering these basics – income, expenses, and savings – you'll build a solid foundation for your financial wellness.

Income: The Financial Fuel

Understanding your income is the first step to financial empowerment. Income includes your salary, bonuses, side hustles, or any money that flows into your pocket. It's essential to know not only the total amount but also its sources and consistency.

Example:

Meet Sarah, a young professional with a monthly salary of $4,000 and an additional $500 from a freelance gig. Understanding her income involves not just acknowledging the total sum but recognizing the stability of her primary income source (salary) and the variability of her freelance income.

Expenses: Where Your Money Goes

To manage your finances effectively, it's crucial to track your expenses. This includes everything from rent and groceries to entertainment and utilities. Categorizing and understanding your spending habits is key to maintaining a balanced financial life.

Example:

Let's revisit Sarah. After categorizing her expenses, she realizes she spends $1,200 on rent, $300 on groceries, $150 on utilities, and $200 on entertainment monthly. Tracking her expenses allows her to identify areas where she can optimize spending.

Savings: Your Financial Safety Net

Savings act as a financial cushion during unexpected events and form the basis of your wealth-building journey. Setting aside a portion of your income regularly is a crucial habit for long-term financial stability.

Example:

Sarah decides to allocate 20% of her monthly income to savings. This means putting away $900 ($400 into an emergency fund, $500 into a long-term savings account). Establishing this habit ensures she's prepared for unforeseen expenses and is actively working towards her financial goals.

Creating a Personalized Budget

Now that you understand income, expenses, and savings, it's time to put this knowledge into action by creating a personalized budget. A budget is your financial roadmap, guiding you towards your goals while keeping you on track.

Example:

Sarah crafts a detailed budget allocating specific amounts to categories like housing, food, utilities, entertainment, and savings. This budget not only ensures that she covers all her expenses but also allows her to allocate funds strategically towards her financial priorities.

In conclusion, mastering the basics of income, expenses, and savings lays the groundwork for financial success. The example of Sarah showcases how applying this knowledge in real life can lead to a more intentional and effective approach to managing finances. As we move forward in "Mastering Your Money," remember that a strong foundation is the key to a resilient and prosperous financial future.

Chapter 2:

Building a Solid Financial Base

Lesson: Establishing Emergency Funds

In this chapter, we'll delve into a crucial aspect of financial stability – establishing emergency funds. Life is unpredictable, and having a financial safety net can make all the difference during unexpected events. Let's explore why emergency funds are vital and how to build and maintain them.

Understanding the Importance of Emergency Funds

Why Have an Emergency Fund?

- Unforeseen Expenses: From sudden medical bills to car repairs, life is filled with unexpected expenses.

- Job Loss or Income Reduction: A robust emergency fund provides a financial buffer during periods of unemployment or reduced income.

Example:

Meet Alex, a young professional who diligently saves six months' worth of living expenses in an emergency fund. When unexpected medical expenses arise, Alex taps into the emergency fund without derailing long-term financial goals. This financial cushion allows Alex to navigate the challenge without accumulating debt or jeopardizing other financial priorities.

How to Build and Maintain Your Emergency Fund

1. Set a Goal: Determine the amount you want to save based on your monthly living expenses and individual circumstances.

2. Consistent Contributions: Allocate a portion of your income to your emergency fund regularly. Treat it as a non-negotiable expense.

3. Choose the Right Account: Keep your emergency fund in a separate, easily accessible account, such as a high-yield savings account.

4. Review and Adjust: Periodically reassess your living expenses and adjust your emergency fund goal as needed. Adjust your financial plans to accommodate shifts in life circumstances.

Example:

Emily, a recent graduate, decides to start her emergency fund. She sets a goal of $5,000, equivalent to three months' worth of living expenses. By consistently saving $200 each month, she achieves her goal in two years. When her car unexpectedly breaks down, Emily is relieved to have her emergency fund, preventing financial stress and allowing her to address the situation promptly.

Real-life Scenarios: The Impact of Having or Lacking an Emergency Fund

1. Having an Emergency Fund:

Scenario: Mary, a freelancer, experiences a sudden drop in client projects.

Impact: With her emergency fund, Mary can cover her essential expenses while actively seeking new projects, preventing financial strain.

2. Lacking an Emergency Fund:

Scenario: John, without an emergency fund, faces unexpected home repairs.

Impact: Forced to rely on credit cards or loans, John accumulates debt, paying more in the long run and jeopardizing his financial well-being.

In conclusion, establishing and maintaining an emergency fund is a cornerstone of financial stability. Real-life examples demonstrate how having or lacking an emergency fund can significantly impact your ability to weather unexpected financial storms. As we proceed in "Mastering Your Money," remember that an emergency fund is not just a financial tool; it's your ticket to peace of mind in the face of uncertainty.

Chapter 3:

Investing for Long-Term Growth

Lesson: Introduction to Investing

Welcome to the exciting world of investing, where we'll explore various investment options, assess risk tolerance, and delve into the art of building a diversified portfolio. Investing can be a powerful tool for long-term growth and wealth accumulation when approached with knowledge and strategy.

Understanding Investment Options

1. Stocks: Owning shares of a company gives you a stake in its success and potential dividends.

2. Bonds: Considered safer than stocks, bonds are debt securities that pay periodic interest.

3. Mutual Funds: Pools of money from multiple investors are invested in a diversified portfolio of stocks, bonds, or other securities.

4. Real Estate: Investing in properties for rental income or capital appreciation.

Example:

Jennifer is considering investing $10,000. After researching, she decides on a diversified approach. She allocates 40% to a stock index fund, 30% to bonds, and 30% to a real estate investment trust (REIT). This balanced portfolio aims to maximize potential returns while managing risk.

Assessing Risk Tolerance

1. Risk Capacity: Evaluate your financial ability to absorb potential losses without jeopardizing your goals.

2. Risk Tolerance: Understand your emotional comfort with risk. Some investments fluctuate more than others.

3. Investment Horizon: Consider your time horizon. Longer investment periods can generally withstand more market volatility.

Example:

Mark, in his 30s with a stable job and a long-term investment horizon, has a higher risk tolerance. He allocates a larger portion of his investment portfolio to stocks, aiming for higher potential returns over time.

Building a Diversified Portfolio

1. Spread Across Asset Classes: Allocate investments across different asset classes to minimize risk.

2. Re-balance Regularly: Periodically review and adjust your portfolio to maintain desired asset allocations.

3. Stay Informed: Keep abreast of market trends and economic conditions to make informed investment decisions.

Example:

Lisa builds a diversified portfolio by investing in a mix of U.S. and international stocks, government bonds, and real estate. As the market evolves, she periodically re-balances her portfolio to ensure it aligns with her financial goals and risk tolerance.

Calculating Returns and Risks

1. Returns: Evaluate potential returns based on historical performance, market conditions, and investment goals.

2. Risks: Consider potential downsides, market volatility, and external factors influencing investments.

Example:

Michael invests $5,000 in a technology stock with an expected annual return of 8% and a government bond with a 4% return. By calculating potential returns and considering associated risks, he can make informed decisions aligning with his investment objectives.

In conclusion, this lesson introduces you to the diverse realm of investments. By exploring various options, understanding risk tolerance, and building a diversified portfolio, you lay the groundwork for long-term growth. The provided examples illustrate the practical application of these concepts, allowing you to embark on your investment journey with confidence. As we move forward in "Mastering Your Money," remember that investing is a dynamic and evolving process, requiring ongoing education and strategic decision-making.

Chapter 4:

Conquering Debt

Lesson: Strategies for Debt Repayment

Welcome to a crucial chapter in your financial journey – conquering debt. In this chapter, we'll delve into understanding different debt types and implementing effective strategies to repay them. By mastering these strategies, you'll gain control over your finances and pave the way for a more secure financial future.

Understanding Different Debt Types

1. Credit Card Debt: High-interest debt often accumulated from credit card usage.

2. Student Loans: Loans taken for educational purposes with varying interest rates.

3. Mortgages: Long-term loans for purchasing homes, typically with lower interest rates.

4. Personal Loans: Unsecured loans with fixed or variable interest rates.

Example:

Emily has credit card debt with an interest rate of 18%, a student loan at 5%, and a mortgage at 4%. Understanding the different interest rates and structures helps Emily prioritize repayment strategies.

Implementing Effective Debt Repayment Strategies

1. Snowball Method: Start by paying off the smallest debt first, gaining momentum as you tackle larger debts.

2. Avalanche Method: Prioritize debts with the highest interest rates, minimizing overall interest payments.

3. Debt Consolidation: Combine multiple debts into a single loan with a lower interest rate.

4. Balance Transfers: Transfer high-interest credit card balances to cards with lower rates.

Example:

John, facing credit card debt, student loans, and a car loan, chooses the avalanche method. He prioritizes paying off the credit card debt with the highest interest rate first, then tackles other debts systematically. This strategic approach saves John money on interest payments in the long run.

Creating a Debt Repayment Plan

1. List all Debts: Compile a comprehensive list of all outstanding debts, including amounts and interest rates.

2. Assess Financial Situation: Evaluate your budget and identify areas where you can allocate additional funds towards debt repayment.

3. Set Realistic Goals: Define achievable milestones for debt repayment based on your financial capacity.

Example:

Sarah creates a debt repayment plan, listing her credit card debt, student loans, and car loan. Assessing her budget, she allocates an extra $200 per month towards debt repayment. Setting a realistic goal, Sarah plans to eliminate her credit card debt within six months.

Analyzing the Impact on Overall Financial Health

1. Improved Credit Score: Timely debt repayment positively influences your credit score.

2. Financial Freedom: Reducing debt liberates funds for saving, investing, and pursuing long-term goals.

3. Stress Reduction: A structured debt repayment plan alleviates financial stress, promoting overall well-being.

Example:

Mark successfully repays his high-interest credit card debt using the debt snowball method. As a result, his credit score improves, and he experiences reduced financial stress. This newfound financial freedom allows Mark to redirect funds towards building an emergency fund and investing for the future.

In conclusion, conquering debt requires a combination of understanding different debt types and implementing effective repayment strategies. The provided example illustrates how creating a debt repayment plan and strategically addressing debts positively impact overall financial health. As you apply these strategies in "Mastering Your Money," remember that tackling debt is a powerful step towards financial freedom and a more secure financial future.

Chapter 5:

Mastering Credit

Lesson: Navigating the Credit Landscape

Welcome to the world of credit mastery. In this chapter, we'll unravel the complexities of credit scores, delve into responsible credit management, and explore ways to enhance your creditworthiness. Understanding the nuances of credit is essential for making informed financial decisions and unlocking favorable opportunities.

Deciphering Credit Scores

1. What is a Credit Score: A numerical representation of your creditworthiness, typically ranging from 300 to 850.

2. Factors Influencing Credit Scores: Payment history, credit utilization, length of credit history, types of credit in use, and new credit.

Example:

Emily checks her credit score and discovers it's 750. Understanding the factors that contribute to her score, such as timely payments and a diverse credit history, empowers Emily to maintain and improve her credit standing.

Managing Credit Responsibly

1. Timely Payments: Pay all bills on time to maintain a positive payment history.

2. Credit Utilization: Keep credit card balances low compared to credit limits to demonstrate responsible credit use.

3. Diverse Credit Portfolio: Maintain a mix of credit types, such as credit cards, installment loans, and retail accounts.

Example:

John consistently pays his credit card bills on time, avoids maxing out credit limits, and has a mix of credit types. As a result, John establishes a solid credit history, positively influencing his credit score.

Improving Creditworthiness

1. Check Your Credit Report: Regularly review your credit report for inaccuracies and address any discrepancies.

2. Address Negative Items: Work to resolve any late payments, defaults, or other negative items on your credit report.

3. Be Patient: Building or improving credit takes time, so be patient and consistent with positive credit behaviors.

Example:

Sarah discovers an error on her credit report. By disputing and resolving the issue, she improves her creditworthiness, leading to a higher credit score and more favorable financial opportunities.

Exploring the Impact of a Good Credit Score

1. Lower Interest Rates: Lenders often offer lower interest rates to individuals with higher credit scores.

2. Access to Better Financial Products: A good credit score opens doors to premium credit cards, favorable loan terms, and competitive interest rates.

Example:

Mark, with an excellent credit score of 800, applies for a mortgage. Due to his high creditworthiness, he secures a lower interest rate compared to someone with a lower credit score. Over the life of the loan, Mark saves a substantial amount on interest payments.

In conclusion, mastering credit involves deciphering credit scores, managing credit responsibly, and actively working to improve creditworthiness. The example illustrates how a good credit score can lead to tangible financial benefits, emphasizing the importance of maintaining a healthy credit profile. As you navigate the credit landscape in "Mastering Your Money," remember that credit is a valuable financial tool that, when wielded wisely, can enhance your financial well-being.

Chapter 6:

Advanced Saving Techniques

Lesson: Maximizing Savings

Welcome to the realm of advanced saving techniques, where we'll explore strategies that go beyond the basics. By incorporating advanced methods like utilizing tax-advantaged accounts and implementing automated savings plans, you can elevate your savings game and accelerate your path to financial goals.

Exploring Advanced Saving Strategies

1. Tax-Advantaged Accounts: Take advantage of accounts that offer tax benefits, such as 401(k)s, IRAs, and Health Savings Accounts (HSAs).

2. Automated Savings Plans: Set up automatic transfers to savings accounts to ensure consistent contributions without manual effort.

Example:

Alex, aiming to maximize savings, contributes to his employer's 401(k) for retirement (pre-tax contributions) and utilizes an HSA for medical expenses. Additionally, he sets up automated transfers to a high-yield savings account, effortlessly building his emergency fund.

Tax-Advantaged Accounts: A Strategic Approach

1. 401(k) and IRA Contributions: Contribute to retirement accounts, taking advantage of tax benefits and potential employer matches.

2. Health Savings Accounts (HSAs): Leverage HSAs for tax-free contributions and withdrawals for qualified medical expenses.

Example:

Emily contributes $6,000 annually to her Traditional IRA, taking advantage of pre-tax contributions. She also allocates a portion of her income to an HSA, benefiting from tax-free contributions and withdrawals for medical expenses.

Automated Savings Plans: Consistency is Key

1. Set Clear Goals: Define specific savings goals, such as an emergency fund, a travel fund, or a down payment fund.

2. Automatic Transfers: Schedule recurring transfers to your savings accounts on payday to ensure consistent contributions.

Example:

Mark establishes an automated savings plan, directing a portion of his salary each month to a separate travel fund. Over time, he accumulates the necessary funds for his dream vacation without feeling the financial strain.

Calculating the Potential Growth of Savings

1. Compound Interest: Understand the power of compound interest, where your savings earn interest on both the principal and previously earned interest.

2. Time Horizon: The longer your money is invested or saved, the greater the impact of compound interest.

Example:

Sarah starts saving $300 per month in an investment account with an average annual return of 7%. Over 20 years, her initial investment grows substantially due to the compounding effect, showcasing the importance of a long-term perspective in maximizing savings.

In conclusion, advanced saving techniques involve leveraging tax-advantaged accounts and implementing automated savings plans. The example demonstrates how a strategic approach, combined with the power of compound interest, can significantly enhance the growth of your savings. As you dive into advanced saving strategies in "Mastering Your Money," remember that consistency, thoughtful planning, and a long-term mindset are key elements of successful wealth accumulation.

Chapter 7:

Planning for Retirement

Lesson: Retirement Planning Essentials

Embark on a journey towards a financially secure future as we explore retirement planning essentials. In this chapter, we'll delve into understanding retirement accounts, setting realistic retirement goals, and crafting a plan that ensures your golden years are comfortable and worry-free.

Understanding Retirement Accounts

1. 401(k) and 403(b): Employer-sponsored retirement plans allowing pre-tax contributions and potential employer matches.

2. Individual Retirement Accounts (IRAs): Personal retirement accounts providing tax advantages for contributions.

3. Roth IRAs: Tax-free withdrawals in retirement for qualified distributions.

Example:

John, in his mid-30s, contributes to his employer's 401(k), taking advantage of both pre-tax contributions and employer matches. He also opens a Roth IRA to diversify his retirement savings and enjoy tax-free withdrawals in retirement.

Setting Realistic Retirement Goals

1. Evaluate Lifestyle: Consider the lifestyle you desire in retirement, factoring in living expenses, travel, and leisure activities.

2. Assess Time Horizon: Determine the number of years until retirement, influencing your investment strategy and savings targets.

Example:

Emily envisions a comfortable retirement with regular travel. Assessing her time horizon (25 years until retirement), she calculates the funds needed to support her desired lifestyle, guiding her savings goals.

The Power of Early Retirement Contributions

1. Compounding Effect: Understand how early contributions benefit from the compounding effect over time.

2. Long-Term Growth: Contributions made in the early years have more time to grow, amplifying their impact.

Example:

Mark starts contributing $500 per month to his retirement account at age 25. By the time he reaches 65, the compounding effect has significantly increased his retirement savings compared to someone who starts contributing the same amount at age 35, emphasizing the advantage of early contributions.

Retirement Savings Projection: A Practical Example

1. Assumptions: Use realistic assumptions for investment returns, inflation, and retirement age.

2. Regular Assessments: Periodically reassess your projections based on changes in income, expenses, and investment performance.

Example:

Sarah, at 40, creates a retirement savings projection. With conservative assumptions and a diligent savings plan, she projects having a substantial nest egg by her planned retirement age of 65, giving her confidence in her ability to retire comfortably.

In conclusion, mastering retirement planning involves understanding various retirement accounts, setting realistic goals, and harnessing the power of early contributions. The provided example illustrates the impact of early retirement contributions on long-term savings. As you engage in retirement planning in "Mastering Your Money," remember that careful consideration, regular assessments, and proactive contributions are vital components of securing a financially sound retirement.

Chapter 8:

Tax Optimization Strategies

Lesson: Navigating the Tax Code

Welcome to the intricate world of tax optimization. In this chapter, we'll explore strategies for maximizing tax efficiency through deductions, credits, and strategic financial planning. Understanding the tax code and implementing savvy strategies can significantly impact your overall financial outcomes.

Maximizing Tax Efficiency

1. Tax Deductions: Identify eligible deductions to reduce taxable income, such as mortgage interest, student loan interest, and charitable contributions.

2. Tax Credits: Utilize credits, like the Child Tax Credit or Education Credits, to directly reduce your tax liability.

Example:

Emily strategically plans her charitable contributions, taking advantage of the tax deduction for donations. Additionally, she qualifies for education credits by financing her continued education, optimizing both deductions and credits.

Navigating the Tax Code: Key Considerations

1. Understanding Marginal Tax Rates: Be aware of how tax rates increase with income, helping you evaluate the impact of deductions.

2. Timing of Deductions: Strategically time deductions to maximize benefits, such as bundling charitable contributions in high-income years.

Example:

John, with a variable income, coordinates his deductible expenses in years with higher earnings, effectively lowering his overall tax liability and maximizing savings.

Smart Financial Planning for Tax Efficiency

1. Retirement Contributions: Contribute to tax-advantaged retirement accounts, reducing taxable income while saving for the future.

2. Investment Strategies: Implement tax-efficient investment strategies, such as holding investments for the long term to benefit from lower capital gains rates.

Example:

Mark strategically allocates his investments, prioritizing tax-efficient funds in his taxable accounts and tax-advantaged accounts for investments with higher expected returns, optimizing his overall tax position.

Analyzing the Impact of Tax-Saving Strategies

1. Before and After Analysis: Assess your financial situation both before and after implementing tax-saving strategies to quantify the impact.

2. Long-Term Planning: Consider the cumulative impact of tax-saving strategies on long-term financial goals.

Example:

Sarah, by maximizing retirement contributions and strategically managing deductions, analyzes her overall financial outcomes. The impact is substantial, resulting in increased savings for both short-term goals and long-term objectives like retirement.

In conclusion, navigating the tax code involves a nuanced understanding of deductions, credits, and smart financial planning. The example provided illustrates how tax-saving strategies can significantly influence overall financial outcomes. As you explore tax optimization in "Mastering Your Money," remember that staying informed, strategic planning, and adapting to changes in tax laws are essential components of maximizing tax efficiency and enhancing your financial well-being.

Chapter 9:

Setting and Achieving Financial Goals

Lesson: Goal Setting for Financial Success

Welcome to a pivotal chapter in your financial journey. In this chapter, we'll delve into the art of setting realistic financial goals and crafting actionable plans to achieve them. Understanding how to establish and pursue your objectives is fundamental to your overall financial success.

Establishing Realistic Financial Goals

1. Short-Term Goals: Focus on objectives you can achieve within the next 1-3 years, such as building an emergency fund or paying off high-interest debt.

2. Mid-Term Goals: Look ahead 3-5 years for goals like saving for a down payment on a home or funding a significant vacation.

3. Long-Term Goals: Plan for goals that require 5 years or more, such as retirement planning or funding your children's education.

Example:

Emily sets short-term goals to eliminate credit card debt, mid-term goals to save for a down payment on a home, and long-term goals for retirement planning. Each goal aligns with her financial priorities and time horizon.

Creating Actionable Plans

1. Define Clear Objectives: Clearly articulate what you want to achieve with each financial goal.

2. Break Down Goals: Divide larger goals into smaller, manageable steps to make progress more achievable.

3. Allocate Resources: Identify the financial resources required for each goal and allocate your income strategically.

Example:

John aims to start a small business within the next five years. His actionable plan includes steps like researching the market, saving a specific amount each month for startup costs, and acquiring necessary skills through courses or workshops.

Developing a Step-by-Step Plan for Major Milestones

1. Identify Major Milestones: Break down significant goals into key milestones to track progress.

2. Timeline for Achievement: Set realistic timelines for each milestone, considering external factors and potential challenges.

Example:

Mark plans to save $50,000 for a major investment property purchase within the next three years. His step -by-step plan involves saving a specific amount each month, reassessing his progress quarterly, and adjusting the plan if necessary.

Regularly Assessing and Adjusting Goals

1. Review Progress: Regularly assess your progress towards each goal to stay on track.

2. Adjust Goals as Needed: Life circumstances change, and it's essential to adjust your goals and plans accordingly.

Example:

Sarah initially planned to pay off her student loans in five years but experienced a career change. She reassesses her financial situation, adjusts her timeline, and creates a new plan aligned with her current circumstances.

In conclusion, setting and achieving financial goals involves a thoughtful and strategic approach. The example provided illustrates the importance of developing a step -by - step plan for major milestones, highlighting the practical application of goal-setting principles. As you navigate this lesson in "Mastering Your Money," remember that flexibility, regular assessments, and adaptability are key elements in achieving financial success.

Chapter 10:

Mindful Spending and Lifestyle Choices

Lesson: Cultivating Financial Awareness

As we conclude our journey in "Mastering Your Money," let's explore the art of mindful spending and lifestyle choices. This final chapter emphasizes the importance of aligning your spending decisions with long-term financial objectives. Cultivating financial awareness is key to achieving a harmonious balance between your current lifestyle and future financial aspirations.

Making Mindful Spending Decisions

1. Evaluate Needs vs. Wants: Distinguish between essential expenses and discretionary spending to prioritize your financial well-being.

2. Budgeting for Enjoyment: Allocate funds for leisure and entertainment while ensuring it aligns with your overall financial plan.

Example:

Emily identifies her needs, such as housing and utilities, and distinguishes them from wants, like dining out frequently. By budgeting for both necessities and enjoyment, she strikes a balance that supports her financial goals.

Analyzing the Financial Impact of Lifestyle Choices

1. Evaluate Long-Term Costs: Consider the financial consequences of lifestyle choices, such as upgrading to a larger home or purchasing a luxury vehicle.

2. Opportunity Costs: Understand that every financial decision involves trade-offs, and consider the potential benefits and drawbacks.

Example:

John contemplates upgrading to a larger home. By analyzing the long-term costs, including increased mortgage payments and maintenance expenses, he weighs these against the benefits of additional space, making an informed decision aligned with his financial objectives.

Demonstrating the Benefits of Conscious Spending

1. Financial Freedom: Mindful spending leads to financial freedom, allowing you to allocate funds toward savings, investments, and meaningful experiences.

2. Reduced Stress: Being intentional about spending reduces financial stress, promoting overall well-being.

Example:

Mark practices conscious spending by focusing on experiences over material possessions. This not only enhances his overall satisfaction but also allows him to redirect funds towards building an emergency fund and investing for the future.

Integrating Mindful Spending into Daily Life

1. Regular Financial Check-Ins: Schedule regular reviews of your budget and spending patterns to stay on track.

2. Aligning Spending with Values: Ensure your spending aligns with your values and long-term goals.

Example:

Sarah incorporates regular financial check-ins into her routine. By consistently reviewing her spending and aligning it with her values, she creates a financial lifestyle that supports her aspirations.

In conclusion, cultivating financial awareness through mindful spending and lifestyle choices is the pinnacle of financial mastery. The example provided illustrates how analyzing the financial impact of choices and demonstrating the benefits of conscious spending can lead to a more fulfilling and financially secure future. As you apply these principles in "Mastering Your Money," remember that every financial decision is a step towards your desired future, and by cultivating awareness, you empower yourself to make choices that align with your financial goals.

Conclusion:

Mastering Your Money

Congratulations on reaching the final pages of "Mastering Your Money"! This journey has equipped you with essential financial tips, lessons, and real-world examples to navigate the complex landscape of personal finance. As you close this chapter, let's reflect on the principles that will empower you to take control of your financial destiny.

Your Financial Journey

Financial success is not a static destination; it's an ongoing journey. By embracing the principles outlined in this book, you've laid the foundation for a resilient and prosperous financial future. Remember that each decision, whether big or small, contributes to your overall financial well-being.

Applying the Principles

Apply the principles you've learned consistently. Create a budget that aligns with your goals, make informed investment decisions, conquer debt strategically, and leverage the power of compounding for long-term growth. The art of setting and achieving financial goals, navigating the tax code, and making mindful spending decisions will guide you on this path.

Discipline and Patience

Financial success requires discipline and patience. Rome wasn't built in a day, and similarly, your wealth will grow gradually. Stay committed to your financial plan, make adjustments as needed, and remember that the journey is just as important as the destination.

Building a Secure Future

As you implement these principles, envision the secure and abundant future you are cultivating. An emergency fund stands ready for unforeseen challenges, investments steadily grow, and retirement plans take shape. The impact of conscious spending echoes in a life enriched by experiences rather than mere possessions.

Empowering Yourself

Financial literacy is a powerful tool, and you've equipped yourself with the knowledge needed to make informed decisions. Whether it's understanding the nuances of credit, optimizing taxes, or crafting a detailed budget, you now possess the skills to navigate the complexities of your financial landscape.

Moving Forward with Confidence

As you move forward, remember that financial success is not about perfection but progress. Life is dynamic, and your financial plan should evolve with it. Embrace change, stay informed, and continue educating yourself. Your newfound financial confidence will empower you to adapt and thrive in an ever-changing financial landscape.

A Journey to Prosperity

"Mastering Your Money" is not just a book; it's a guide for a journey towards prosperity and financial freedom. Your commitment to financial mastery positions you as the architect of your financial destiny. Keep the lessons close, share your knowledge, and inspire others on their journey to financial well-being.

Wishing you a future filled with financial abundance, security, and the freedom to live life on your terms. May your journey be fulfilling, and may you continue to master your money with confidence and purpose.

<u>NOTES</u>